They Eat Dirt, Don't They?

and other hilarious truths of family life

**from the pages of
Christian Parenting Today
magazine**

Christian Parenting Books is an imprint of Chariot Family Publishing,
a div. of David C. Cook Publishing Co.
David C. Cook Publishing Co., Elgin, Illinois 60120
David C. Cook Publishing Co., Weston, Ontario
Nova Distribution Ltd., Newton Abbot, England

Christian Parenting Today Magazine
P.O. Box 850, Sisters, OR 97759 (800) 238-2221

THEY EAT DIRT, DON'T THEY?
©1993 by Chariot Family Publishing

Cover art by Greg Cross
Compiled and edited by Colin Miller

First Printing, 1993
Printed in the United States of America
97 96 95 94 93 5 4 3 2 1

ISBN 0-78140-144-5

They Eat Dirt, Don't They?

and other hilarious truths of family life

from the pages of
Christian Parenting Today
magazine

compiled and edited by
Colin Miller

illustrated by
Greg Cross

Christian Parenting BOOKS

Table of Contents

Editor's Introduction

In my three-plus years of magazine making at *Christian Parenting Today*, I've noticed others on the staff fussing and laboring, producing well-researched and painstakingly edited articles.

Meanwhile, I've been in my office cackling over cartoons, humorous features and reader-contributed anecdotes. So the job of compiling all this hilarity fell, happily, to me.

These light-hearted articles were originally meant to be encouraging diversions, breathing room for readers in danger of being overwhelmed by hard facts and brilliant advice.

Fortunately, the humor is as well-received by our readers as the rest of the magazine is. It's been a wonderful surprise to find out that great magazines are made from the contributions of inspired parents as much as they are from the work of all our doctorate-wielding writers and eloquent experts.

This book is compiled from the first five years of *Christian Parenting Today*. I hope you have as much fun reading it as I've had putting it together.

Colin

Colin Miller
Associate Editor

Foreword

by Marti Attoun

Raising children is hard work and parents need a recess now and then. That's why God created VBS, church camps, teen retreats, lock-ins and nursery workers with big purses brimming with graham crackers.

That's why we created this little book. When you need a humor break, sneak a peek at these anecdotes, cartoons and stories. A peek a day will revive your smile.

Some parents may not recognize when they need a revival, so here are some telling signs. You need a break if you've ever thought or said any of these phrases:

• "Don't bother hanging up that shirt. Just throw it on the floor."

• "Bring that newt to the table. He's hungry, too."

• "Kids, turn on the water sprinkler and do some mud wrestling while I'm gone."

• "I've got a great idea. Why don't you invite all your friends over for pizza? Might as well have them spend the night, too."

• "Here are the car keys. Gas tank's full."

• "From now on, I'm going to give you $5 a week allowance for remembering to breathe."

• "Son, with that purple hair, you look just like your grandmother."

• "These pumps are only $92? I can buy a second pair to wear for creek shoes."

• "Is that as loud as you can twang that electric guitar?"

• "Lower those bangs into your eyes. It'll keep you from getting sunburned."

• "You don't watch enough TV. We'd better sign up for HBO."

• "Another A in science? You're obviously studying too hard and neglecting your social skills."

• "Latest medical news flash. Eat corn dogs and candy bars as part of a well-balanced breakfast."

• "Please crank up that volume so I can hear MTV while I'm in the shower."

• "Don't forget to close my purse after you take all my money."

• "It's minus 20°, but don't wear that stocking cap. Your hair might get smashed."

• "And speaking of hair, could you stand in front of the bathroom mirror another hour, please? I'm worried that you missed spraying a hair or two."

If you found yourself saying any of these phrases, start reading this book immediately. You need a parenting break. Maybe some graham crackers, too.

"Two hundred and *twenty*!"

A Child's-Eye View

("Did you know your nostrils look enormous?")

They Eat Dirt, Don't They?

Some folks obviously haven't spent much time with normal, mud-blooded kids.

by Jeanne Zornes

I couldn't believe it was "news." Yet, there it was, complete with photo and map, wedged between luggage and health spa ads on page four of a highbrow, big-city daily.

The paper had sent a reporter halfway across the nation, to the heartland of Mississippi, to confirm a rumor that people there actually ate dirt. The reporter called it by its scientific name, "geophagy," and described the highway dirt-bank where locals scooped up bucketfuls of the stuff for snacking.

As the mother of young children, I was not impressed. Obviously the writer and editors hadn't spent much time around normal, mud-blooded kids.

My kids would eat dirt, unmentionables from the nose, and (if not intercepted) chewing gum stuck to sidewalks. They also put mustard on cottage cheese and pickles in milk.

When I brought my dimpled wonders home from the hospital, I didn't set out to teach them the finer points of haute cuisine à la natural. With our firstborn, we were typical nervous parents who ran to sterilize any pacifier which suffered chance contamination. And we dutifully purchased the sludge sold as baby food, and coaxed it into a pouting little mouth with time-honored, airplane dive-bomber tactics.

About the time junior started crawling, I suspected a yen for dirt and other dastardly things must come as standard equipment with babies, along with Original Sin. Ours chased dust balls, staples, lint and anything else the vacuum missed.

By the time a little sister arrived, junior had been promoted to outside play with all its delicious temptations—like the flower beds. More than once I answered an urgent call for Mommy, only to discover he (and later his sister) wanted to show off a back-to-nature birthday party, complete with mud cocoa, mud cookies, and mud-and-grass chocolate cake.

"Cookie, Mommy?" my junior chef offered, holding a plate of sun-baked earth in his grubby hands.

"Later, sweetie," I demurred.

11

What I never understood was how these children, a few years later, considered my healthy cooking a conspiracy to destroy their bodies. It was the firstborn (whose first words after "Mama" and "Dada" were "French fries") who developed a near-panic aversion to anything under the heading of "vegetable" or "meat" (except hot dogs).

If I'd asked him what the four basic food groups were, I'm sure he would have answered "cola, candy, cookies and chips."

The table became a battlefield whenever I cooked anything which even vaguely hinted at gourmet.

> **"I never understood how these children, a few years later, considered my cooking a conspiracy to destroy their bodies."**

"I don't like it," wailed junior.

"How do you know you don't like it?" I countered. "You haven't even tried it. One bite, or else."

Three glasses of milk, enough catsup for a Wild West massacre movie, and one micro-bite later, he complained, "I still don't like it."

Finally, to get anything at all between his jaws, I decided to appeal to his primal nature.

"Here's your volcano," I'd chirp, plopping mashed potatoes on his plate. "And now some nice lava for the center," I added, dribbling some gravy in the middle. "Pretend you're a dinosaur and you'll become extinct if you don't eat."

I would have fared better if I'd merely

said, "Here's some white dirt. Now let's pour some mud-water in it."

We believe we may be in for a new phase. The other day I discovered my son, now 7, standing in front of the refrigerator. A great Arctic chill wafted its way across the room.

"Hungry?" I asked casually, hoping he'd grab an apple and go on with life.

He pouted. "There's nothing good in here. When are you going to get us some good food?"

I recalled the dirt-eating folk in the rural South. One lady confided to the reporter that she put dirt over ice cream. Maybe it's worth a try, I thought.

"As near as I can understand it, they're my real mom and dad."

Artistic Flare

Our 2½-year-old daughter, Kelsey, was getting quite good at drawing faces. With each face she drew she added new details. One day I noticed she had drawn a new face, complete with eyes, nose, mouth and two little circles on the nose. We had never really discussed nostrils, so I was curious how she would explain this newest feature.

"Kelsey, what are those?" I asked.

"Those things," she said.

"What things?"

"You know, those things, those things you put your finger in."

TRACY BALZER, REDMOND, WASH.

Good Question

I know that 2-year-olds are supposed to be curious, and that you're supposed to keep up with their questions, but at the end of a long day, my daughter, Lizzie, had the last word:

"Mom, is that your head? Is that your head, Mom? Hey, Mom? Mom? Is that your head, Mom? Is that your head?"

"Yes, it is, Lizzie!"

"Why?"

SUSAN B. NELSON, SCOTTS VALLEY, CALIF.

No Moral to the Story

One evening while saying bedtime prayers, my daughter, Bethany, asked me if it makes Jesus sad when we forget to thank him for what he has done for us. I thought this was a perfect opportunity to tell her the story of how Jesus healed the ten lepers but only one returned to thank him.

Bethany watched me very intently. I thought, "She is really getting a lot out of this story." After I finished, I waited expectantly to hear what she thought of it.

She said, "Mommy, did you realize that when you talk, only your bottom teeth go up and down?"

ELAINE S. WALSH, RICHMOND, VA.

Fearsome Phone Call

One of my neighbor's sociology class assignments was to ask certain career questions of young children. Using me as an intermediary over the telephone, she asked my 4-year-old son, "What do you want to be when you grow up?"

"A policeman."

"If you were a girl, what would you want to be?"

"I don't want to be a girl," he said with worry in his eyes.

"I know," she assured him through me, "but if you were . . ."

He adamantly refused to consider the possibility. When I hung up he looked at me with large eyes and asked, "Was that God?"

LINNEA DENIS, THE DALLES, ORE.

Meteorology Made Simple

The other evening, my husband yelled from outside on the patio, "Is it s'posed to rain tonight?"

"No, Dad," our 2-year-old called back. "It's s'posed to get dark out."

LORI KEDZIE, ROCHELLE, ILL.

15

Compost Cops

To these earth watchers, every eggshell and potato peel is another rotten idea.

by Marti Attoun

"I'm not out to sabotage the compost pile—or the universe. I just get busy and forget."

I felt them staring at me last night while I calmly peeled five potatoes. They were hoping I'd slip up again like I did with the eggshells.

My children have turned into compost police. My environmentally friendly 11-year-old especially has developed an obscene pride about our backyard compost heap.

"OK, who threw away the coffee grounds?" he asked when he sifted the trash. "Mom, you did it again, didn't you? We need those for our compost pile."

I'm not out to sabotage the compost pile—or the universe. I just get busy and forget what goes into the regular trash can, what goes into the sack of aluminums, what goes into the compost trash can, what goes into the glass trash can, and what goes into the bucket that goes to Uncle Ken's country dogs.

Keeping the garbage organized has become a full-time stinky job. And having compost cops ready to pounce on my peelings doesn't help.

The compost cops and their father visit the compost pile each day to see how things are cooking. They discuss the pile as if it's a neighborhood tourist attraction. And, unfortunately, it is becoming quite the (sniff) attraction.

The compost builders strung fencing around four poles and made the compost corral so big that we don't even have a decent spot with sunshine for a garden.

"Even if we don't have a garden, we need the compost pile to enrich the soil," my husband said.

"Besides, it'll help break up the clay."

The compost cops take turns feeding the pile with leaves and fruit and vegetable matter. But that's not good enough.

"We really need to get our hands on some good cow manure for the compost," the eldest composter said.

"Hey, Dad, at least we were able to grab the Christmas tree off the curb before Mom had the trash man haul it off," my daughter said. "Let's be thankful for that."

"Makes you wonder what other good stuff she's thrown away, doesn't it?" he added.

The 11-year-old piped up: "Come to think of it, I ate two bananas last night. What happened to those peelings? I don't remember seeing those in the compost trash can. And that avocado that Dad ate the other night. What happened to its hide?"

Shortly after, they started spying on me. I'm waiting for one of them to get so aggravated he takes over kitchen duties.

I could warm up to that compost pile real fast then.

17

Boring Chore

My children and I were working together on household cleaning when my 4-year-old asked what he could do.

"Go check out your bedroom and see what shape it's in," I instructed.

A few minutes later he returned and reported, "It's still square."

NANCY LeFEBURE, BEREA, OHIO

Growing Like a Weed

Our 9-year-old son does not like to wash his hair. Sunday morning while parting his wet hair, I commented on how fast his hair is growing, and that he needs a haircut.

"No wonder," he grumbled. "You make me water it so often."

ANN MILLER, TUSCOLA, ILL.

Kid Cowboy

When our son David was 3 years old, he wanted to be a cowboy. He had a pair of cowboy boots that he wore everywhere.

One Wednesday night he wore them to church. As he was getting ready to go home, his teacher said, "David, you have your cowboy boots on the wrong feet."

David looked down at his feet, then up to his teacher, and very seriously replied, "These are my feet!"

KAREN SMITH, BIRMINGHAM, MICH.

Runaway Politeness

My sister Sue was trying to teach her 7-year-old son, Joey, manners—particularly when it came to interrupting adult conversations. One afternoon Joey ran into the room while his parents were visiting with Uncle Harold. "Mom . . ." he started.

"Not now, Joey. How many times do I have to tell you not to interrupt?" Sue scolded.

Joey waited impatiently while Uncle Harold finished his story.

"Mom, can I tell you something now?"

When Sue gave him permission he said, "Uncle Harold's car is rolling down the driveway!"

DEBBI WALSH, COLUMBIA, CONN.

"Surprise! While I was at it I watered the plants inside the house, too."

Should Have Stopped Sooner

My parents were involved in an automobile accident. When I explained to my 3-year-old daughter that her grandpa had an accident in his car, she replied, "Why didn't he just stop and use the potty?"

SUE BAEHRENS, WOOSTER, OHIO

ONE "BIGG" HAPPY FAMILY

"Hi, Mom, we're playing barber . . ."

Sibling Arrivals

("You can take my baby brother back now.")

by Marti Attoun

Going Seat-First

Every kid knows the back seat is for babies.

> "The minute a kid graduates from an infant car seat he's a moving target for back-seat phobia."

All three of my children suffer from back-seat phobia—an irrational and persistent fear of having to occupy the back seat of a moving vehicle.

Back-seat phobia is subtle and sneaks in, ever so sweetly, on a congenial parent. The minute a kid graduates from an infant car seat, or begins to form the "fw" sound necessary for fwont seat, he's a moving target for back-seat phobia.

Mom and Dad think it's so cute at first when little honeycakes wants to ride up front like a big person. "You just wants to see the moo-cows better, don't you, doll?" one of the parent/suckers clucks as he or she crawls into the back seat.

Big mistake. Over the next few months, the little passenger will convince you that he can't see a solitary thing from the back seat. He may as well be blind if he's going to be stuck for life in the back seat, he says.

A parent's next big mistake is falling for the old line, "But there isn't any room back here." To hear the kid wail, you'd think a car was built like a triangle and Mom and Dad are hogging the hypotenuse. Of course there isn't as much room in the back seat because the kid just built Disney World back there out of Legos. There's actually been a lot more room in the back since a certain little passenger kicked the back of the front seat until it permanently lodged under the dashboard.

In advanced cases of back-seat phobia, a kid will simply move out of his bedroom and set up permanent residence in the front seat. Our 11-year-old, Joshua, came up missing once during the Saturday morning cartoons. I finally found him staking out the front seat.

"You said we were going for pizza tonight, didn't you?" he asked.

We've tried to curb back-seat phobia by assigning seat schedules, but something always goes haywire. You don't always know in advance that you're taking a weekend trip and one kid will get to reign for 12 hours in the front seat while the others sulk in the back.

We've flipped coins and drawn straws, but that didn't work either—Mom and Dad both ended up in the back seat.

After frustrating years of trying to pinpoint the trio's abhorrence of the back seat, I think I've finally figured it out: The front seat is one step closer to the driver's seat.

The other day I was driving and 9-year-old Abigail was riding in the front seat wearing her smug winner's smile. I came to a stop and noticed her little paw creeping onto the gear shift.

"Just seven more years," she sighed.

"Get into the back seat now," I shouted. "And you can see the moo-cows just fine if you sit on that pile of Legos."

ONE "BIGG" HAPPY FAMILY by Wheeler

Imaginary Playmate

After coming home from a long day at the office, I was met by my 3½-year-old son begging me to go outside and play with him. I told him I was tired and suggested he play with his younger brother.

"No, Dad," he said. "I want to play with a real person."

RICH GUTEKUNST, COVINGTON, LA.

A Second Opinion

When a baby sitter asked my 3-year-old grandson, Daniel, why his little brother was crying so loudly, Daniel answered, "Well, I pushed him off the slide." Sensing trouble, he hastily added, "But really I think it's his molars coming through!"

JUANITA ARROUES, BOISE, IDAHO

Sibling Generosity

A few days after Rachel, our second child, was born, Grandpa came for a visit. He told our firstborn, 4-year-old Noah, that he was taking Rachel home with him.

"No, you're not," Noah exclaimed boldly. "She's ours!"

Grandpa then offered, "I'll give you two candy bars and a lollipop for her."

Noah hesitated for just a moment and replied, "OK."

It seems that every kid has his price.

CINDY BROWN, NEW CARLISLE, OHIO

Goin' Halfsies

Three-year-old Janet and 6-year-old Nancy were standing in the kitchen fighting over their father.

"He's *my* daddy."

"He's *my* daddy!"

Their mother, busy preparing dinner at the time, thought she'd follow wise Solomon's example. Picking up the butcher knife, she held it out and suggested: "Here. I'll just cut him in half."

"No! No!" Janet screamed. Mom thought she'd made her point until Janet continued, "Get a *clean* knife!"

RICKI MITCHELL, RICE LAKE, WIS.

Just Visiting

I spent the months of my pregnancy diligently preparing my 5- and 3-year-old boys for the arrival of our new baby. The boys were smitten with their new brother—they didn't appear at all jealous. But when the baby was 6 weeks old, my 3-year-old let me know I'd left out at least one important detail. "Oh, Mommy, I love the baby so much," he gushed. "I wish we could keep him."

LISA RAY TURNER, RIO RANCHO, N.M.

"You've got to fight! You've got to *want* to get well."

Motherhood Is Not Terminal

(Unless you have kids.)

by Marti Attoun

Mother's Nose Best

Something about this just doesn't smell right.

"I have become chief sniffer of our family. Without my nose, life in our household would quickly sour."

The other morning my husband dangled an expired shirt in front of me. "Here," he said, "can this make it another day?"

I automatically nose-dived into it, sniffed it thoroughly and pointed to a can of Lysol. Then, with my snoot still smarting, the truth suddenly jolted me like a faceful of garlic breath: I have become chief sniffer of our family. Without my nose, life in our household would quickly sour.

I'm not sure how I became the family's bloodhound, but for as long as I can remember, I've been sticking my muzzle into babies' diapers, suspicious leftovers, cartons of milk, curdled cottage cheese and wings of chicken.

My husband has a nose. A substantial one, in fact. Yet mine is the one summoned when our 8-year-old visits her aunt's cows and comes home with fragrant tennis shoes. I'm the nosy detective who determines whether the baby has been gnawing on dog or people biscuits.

The disturbing realization that the family is exploiting my nostrils led me to make a little informal survey of friends that led to an even more alarming fact: Women are the odor decoders in four out of every five households. Without female snouts, the world would rankle with mildewed gym bags, over-ripened socks and leftover tuna.

According to my investigation, this scene is being repeated in 14 million households every hour across the country: A husband flings open the fridge door and announces that something is rotten. The wife automatically thrusts her nose into a corner of the vegetable bin and tracks down a broccoli with more hair than Rapunzel.

"Oh, my gosh, that's disgusting," the husband gushes while pinching his nose.

Here's another typical scene: A cherry pie has turned black and crinkly in the oven and the smoke alarm is blaring.

"Do you smell something burning, dear?" a husband asks. For some reason, he has no confidence in his own nose. It's a perfectly good nose. It just needs to assert itself.

Kids, too, are just as guilty as husbands for not doing their share of the household sniffing. My own 10-year-old son plunged a carton of chocolate milk under my overworked and unappreciated snout the other day.

"Hey, Mom, is this safe to drink?" he asked.

"Can't you pour it into a cup and smell it yourself?" I replied.

"No way. It's too lumpy to pour."

I say it's time for women to stop this second-nature dawn-to-dusk whiffing at every little whipstitch. I informed the family that my schnoz was on vacation and everyone could be responsible for their own odors for a change.

Shortly after my declaration, my husband showed up with a bouquet from the neighbor's yard. I could swear I smelled a rat.

Confessions of a Formerly Cool Mom

She was majorly adored, like, totally way cool ... ya know?
Then her daughter turned 13.

by Nancy Kennedy

I used to be a cool mom. Wore the right clothes. Cuffed my jeans just so. Sported spikey hair. You know, cool stuff. My daughter adored me.

All that's changed now. No, not my clothes or my hair. What's different now is that my daughter's a teenager. As for me, I've fallen into the black hole of coolness—and I can't get out!

I first noticed my lost coolness status the day we went back-to-school shopping. Alison walked at least two store lengths in front of me throughout the entire mall, muttering: "How could she? How could she?"

It seems I made the mistake of announcing to "everyone in the entire state of Florida" that she needed new underwear. To set the record straight, all I did was shout across the store, "I'll meet you in the lingerie department." (I was in housewares at the time and she was looking at shoes.) I didn't know it would be such a big deal.

Let me warn you, to a teenage girl, underwear is a big deal. A "major big deal."

How was I supposed to know? Nobody told me.

Just like nobody told me that moms aren't supposed to meet their daughters at the school bus stop. Excited to hear about her first day of high school, I waited with Alison's little sister, Laura. That was my first mistake. Waving as the bus came around the corner was my second. My biggest mistake was calling out, "Hi, (nickname)." I'd tell you what it is except I promised I'd never, ever repeat it again in public.

Imagine my surprise when she got off the bus and turned to walk the opposite direction from me! Again she muttered: "How could she? How could she?"

I had to chase her all the way home.

"How could you do that to me, Mom?" she cried once I caught up with her. "How would you like it if you were my age and Grandma met you at the bus stop?"

I shuddered. My mom? At the bus stop? I'd die.

"But I'm different," I told her. "I'm cool."

She looked at me and rolled her eyes.

The light bulb went on.

I'm not different—and I'm not cool anymore either. As the mom of a teenage girl, I rank among the lowest of the low on the coolness scale. Somewhere around Wayne Newton and Vic Damone.

I confess, I served grape Kool-Aid in leftover Barbie birthday cups and generic corn chips to Alison and her friends.

I told the mother of the boy she likes (in front of Alison) that I thought her son was handsome. Not only that, but I invited them over to watch home videos of our trip to Disney World.

I had her paged at K mart.

Last week I drove

As the mom of a teenage girl, I rank among the lowest of the low on the coolness scale.

to the drive-thru window at Burger King in my bathrobe. Even though it was dark and nobody saw me, and even though Alison stayed home, she still accuses me of humiliating her.

The list of my transgressions goes on: When I drop her off anywhere, I shout, "Do you have enough money?" Once, shortly after we moved to a new town, I made a major faux pas by adding, "Do you know our phone number?" (She didn't, but of course she didn't want everyone to know.)

I'm guilty of trying to hold her hand in public. Of driving past her school at lunch time and being seen by her friends. Of introducing myself to the school's head cheerleader and suggesting she and Alison get together since we lived in the same neighborhood.

I'm not real anymore either. All I

36

hear these days is, "Mother, get real."

Recently, I polled a panel of experts on the FCM (Formerly Cool Mom) Syndrome. Actually, it was more like a group of high school girls I found at the mall: I offered to buy them French fries and soda if they'd tell me how a once-cool mom could be cool again.

So, for all of you FCMs out there who, like me, are waiting to be told, here's what the experts said:

Rule #1: Be nice to your daughter's friends, but don't talk to them. Don't ask them questions. Never sing in their presence, especially oldies. Don't dance either unless you're a professional and get paid lots of money.

Rule #2: Never mention personal items in public. Go ahead and buy her Clearasil, underwear and deodorant, but never say who they're for or let anyone see you buy them. Play it safe—shop at least 50 miles away.

Rule #3: Never use current slang. Even if something is totally way cool or absolutely to die for, don't say so. Don't use ancient slang either. Never say "far-out," "right-on" or "with-it." And never, ever say "groovy."

Don't wave to anyone. Don't sing to the radio. Don't drive past anyone who might know your daughter. If at all possible, be invisible.

Rule #4: Dress cool, but not too cool. Keep your closet stocked with clothes your daughter can wear—but don't you wear them. You'll look like you're trying to dress like her.

Rule #5: When asked for your totally honest opinion concerning her hair, weight, clothes, nose size, pimples, etc., don't say, "I'm your mother—I love you just the way you are."

Rule #6: When driving, don't have a "Honk if you love easy listening" bumper sticker. Don't honk at anyone else's bumper sticker. Don't honk. Don't wave to anyone. Don't sing to the radio. Don't drive past anyone who might know your daughter. If at all possible, be invisible.

Unfortunately, there's no guarantee you'll regain coolness status by following these rules. Chances are, no matter what you do, you'll be deemed uncool by your daughter.

But there's hope.

We FCMs can comfort each other with this thought: If there's any justice in the world, one day our daughters will have daughters of their own—and then they'll discover they aren't so cool either.

37

ONE "BIGG" HAPPY FAMILY by Rohrter

I LOVE YOU!
I LOVE YOU!
I LOVE YOU!

I COULD JUST HUG YOU LIKE THIS FOR EVER AND EVER AND...

SNIFF SNIFF

HERE, MOM, YOUR TURN.

WELL, NATHAN, ARE YOU READY FOR YOUR BATH?

NO.

WELL, NATHAN, DO YOU WANT TO STAY STINKY AND DIRTY AND AS FAR AWAY FROM A TUB AS YOU CAN GET?

NO.

IT'S ALL IN HOW YOU PHRASE IT.

NO.

Cooking Commendation

After 18 years of marriage and 5 children, I was still trying to get an enthusiastic response over my meal preparation. One day it finally came! After a week of experimenting with home-made muffins, my loving family reluctantly came to the breakfast table. My 3-year-old smeared the butter on his muffin and took the first bite.

"Mmmm," he sang, approvingly.

"See!" I said. "Someone likes my cooking."

To which he immediately said, "Good butter, Mom!"

KATHLEEN ROBISON, LAGUNA NIGUEL, CALIF.

Name That Mom

Three-year-old Jennifer is a darling little chatterbox. She follows me around the house telling stories or just making conversation. One afternoon, I was particularly tired and my tolerance for non-stop chatter was low. I confronted my shadow: "Jenny, you say 'Mommy' every two minutes. Could you please stop saying 'Mommy' all the time?"

She wandered off only to return two minutes later. "Mommy," she began; then she paused. "I mean Nancy, could I have a drink please?"

NANCY JOHNSON, HAYMARKET, VA.

The Name Is . . . Mommy!

Encounter the legend. See her do wonders. Look in her purse.

by Nancy Kennedy

Do you know me?

There's a container of neon pink Silly Slime dumped in the bottom of my purse and a half-eaten squished strawberry Pop Tart in my jacket pocket. I wear baggy sweats with elastic waists. I know every Raffi song by heart. I live for nap time. My heart pounds for Mr. Rogers—he likes me just the way I am.

I wash my children's faces with spit and my thumb. Pick at the dirt behind their ears. Show their rashes to anyone who'll look. Wipe their noses with my shirt.

I'm sure you've seen me at the market. I'm the one with the permanent stain on my shoulder from baby spit up. The one with dirty footprints on my shirt from non-stop kicking by a child sitting in the grocery cart. The one who didn't have an answer to the (loudly) asked question, "Do we have to eat dog food again tonight?"

You've probably seen me at the mall

> **"I eat leftover baby food smeared on toast for breakfast. I live for nap time. My heart pounds for Mr. Rogers."**

trying to maneuver a stroller with a crying baby who's struggling to get out, while chasing another child who can be twelve places at once. I'm the one carrying the worn-out blankie and Cabbage Patch doll that I warned I wouldn't carry. The one shouting: "Don't touch! I said, DON'T TOUCH!" The one muttering, "I'm never doing this again."

You know who I am. I'm the one with the glazed look on my face after answering for the millionth time, "I don't know what worms eat." I consider myself lucky to get a shower by noon.

I eat leftover baby food smeared on toast for breakfast. I drink leftover milk with graham cracker crumbs floating in it. I eat the crusts nobody wants.

You know me. I'm bleary-eyed from being up all night with a teething baby and teary-eyed from worrying about a toddler who refuses to eat. I have a lapful of baby drool and oatmeal in my hair. I can't remember the last time I had a whole night's sleep or a hot cup of coffee. The only book I've read in the past six months is *Good Night Moon*.

I never get to finish a senten—

I love my husband but (yawn) ZZZZZ.

I used to be reasonably intelligent, pondering the deep secrets of the universe. Now I find myself wondering such things as: If Bert and Ernie aren't related, why do they sleep in the same room? And where are their parents?

I remember a time when getting together with friends meant stimulating conversations about current events, about love and the meaning of life. Now we talk for hours about: Which is better—cloth or disposable? Pacifiers or thumbs? Know any good potty training tips? Maybe you've seen me

41

at church. I'm the one with my skirt on backwards or the entire inner facing of my dress hanging out. In my rush to get everybody dressed, I often forget to check my own appearance.

I know you don't know my first name—I don't have one anymore. I answer to any child calling, "Mom, Mommy, Mama and WAAAAAHHH!!" To be honest, I don't even remember my first name—I've stopped using it myself. When speaking, I simply refer to myself as "Mommy."

"Mommy says to stop poking the cat's ears."

"Mommy's ears can't hear whining."

"Yes, Mommy's wearing her angry face."

"Do you want Mommy to use the spanking spoon?"

I have my good days. Days when we get through breakfast without Cream of Rice on the wall. Days when the cat doesn't end up in the toilet. Days when everyone takes a nap at the same time.

On those days, I feel powerful. In control.

I can nurse a baby and cook dinner at the same time. I can nurse a baby, read a magazine and tie shoes at the same time. I can even nurse a baby and talk on the phone and fold laundry and watch Oprah all at the same time.

You know who I am.

I am mommy. And I don't even need an American Express Card to prove it.

"Ed! I just gave Jimmy's face a good scrubbing and guess what? It's not Jimmy!"

My Perfect Day

by Karen Harter

I awake to the aroma of freshly ground coffee and spring from bed, anticipating another perfect day. As usual, I spend the next half-hour doing my advanced aerobic workout. I am a graceful gazelle. Ah, it's great to be alive.

After a shower and breakfast of quiche and grapefruit, I skim the *New York Times* and the *Wall Street Journal*. Sometimes I write a poem or a letter to my congressman.

My husband steps out of the bathroom wearing nothing but a towel and little beads of water. He looks like something sculpted by Michelangelo. This is obviously a man who has been served only the finest fare; there's just something polyunsaturated about him. He finds his socks in the sock drawer all by himself, and dresses for work. After neatly folding his pajamas and depositing his wet towel in the hamper, he joins me for coffee and meaningful conversation.

Gazing out at our immaculate lawn and

I have a dream. The new day yawns, stretching its golden arms of light through my smudgeless kitchen window. Fresh flowers adorn the table, and there is not a crumb in sight . . .

gardens, we discuss our home, the children, our future. He asks me how I believe the turn of events in Eastern Europe will influence end-time events. My comments are brief, but well-reasoned, and once again he is amazed at my insight and knowledge of the Scriptures and world affairs.

With a tender good-bye kiss, he presses something into my hand, and as he drives out of sight I read the scrawled note: "Anthony's Restaurant on the Bay, 7 P.M. Wear your red dress."

By now the children have rubbed their little eyes and wandered out to the kitchen. I notice that they are already dressed in darling matching outfits, and their hair is combed. Big brother helps little brother into his chair and asks if there is anything he can do to help with breakfast. He carefully empties the Wheaties into two bowls. There is a big, suitable-for-framing picture of Michael Jordan on the cereal box. The two boys eye the one box. Finally, little brother pushes the box across the table.

"You can have it."

"No, you take it . . . I insist," answers his brother with sincere generosity.

The clamor of angry voices from the other bedroom invades my flawless dream. "Mom! Michael wet his bed, and now he's getting into mine!"

"Oh, just a few more minutes," I mumble. I try to go back to my dream, but it has escaped. Reality seeps in through reluctant eyes as I fumble for my old faithful sweat pants.

My husband is missing. The laundry basket has been dumped onto the bedroom floor and clothes are scattered, as if someone were looking for something.

There is a puddle and a wet towel on the bathroom floor, and by the hairy evidence on the counter I deduce that the culprit has trimmed his beard. I wipe up the mess with a frown.

Upon further investigation, I am relieved to see that the suspect left a note. It is stuck to a melon with a toothpick.

"Honey: My lunchbox got ran over by a backhoe. Please pick up a new one. Remember the phone bill. Love, me."

"Mom! Michael wet his bed, and now he's getting into mine!"

OK. So I didn't get up in time to have a romantic interlude with my husband. The day is still young.

I get breakfast on the table for the children, then sneak away to a corner of the living room with a Bible.

The phone rings. It's the church secretary, wondering if I have a committee report ready for her to type up today. I haven't even written it yet. I slink back to my corner and open the Bible.

"Mom, you better come see what Mikey is doing!" warns a voice from the kitchen. I enter in time to see a gallon jug of milk tottering in Michael's arms. I dive. The save is spectacular enough to warrant an instant replay.

The phone rings again. It's my dear friend Emily, who has five children and needs a break and wonders if I can watch her kids this afternoon. "Can I call you back?" I ask. She really has a lot of nerve . . . having five kids, I mean.

Finally, I tune in the morning workout on Channel 15 and plop down at the table with a cup of coffee. I pour syrup on the kids' leftover waffles. (Well, I can't just let them go to waste!) Mikey wanders past, dragging a dripping stuffed raccoon. "I washed Bandit in the toiwet," he announces with pride. I don't even blink. I just take another bite while staring numbly at Miss Perfect-Body, who is disgustingly cheerful and keeps insisting that we do "just one more."

It is 10 A.M. and I am still unshowered and uncombed. I am on my hands and knees scrubbing jam off the linoleum, while mentally stewing my husband for not leaving me the checkbook so I can pay the bills.

Through the hand prints on the sliding glass door I see two brown legs. They are attached to a handsome UPS man who is looking down at me with an amused, Dennis Quaid sort of smirk.

I hate that. He probably thinks I am a messy, disorganized, undisciplined housewife. Oh yes, I know what he's thinking. He's thinking my bangs are too short, and my children are unkempt, and those curtains look tacky with that wallpaper.

I draw myself up with what dignity I can summon, sign for the package and send the still-smirking courier on his way.

"Oh, Lord," I sigh, as the brown truck disappears from the drive. "I try so hard . . ."

My standards are high. I aspire for a model husband, clean, well-behaved children and a home that could, at a moment's notice, grace the cover of *House Beautiful*. Above all, despite numerous unsuccessful attempts, I expect myself to be consistently witty, efficient and cellulite-free. I am failing miserably.

"If only my family would be more cooperative . . . If only there weren't so many interruptions . . ." I glance at my reflection in the glass. "If only I were more perfect."

A hush falls in my spirit. I recognize the strong, quiet voice that whispers, "And what does the Lord require of you, but to do justly, and to love mercy, and to walk humbly with your God." In the momentary stillness, I bask in the simple truth sinking through me.

The Lord will not be coming through the house tonight with a clipboard, checking off my accomplishments, noting imperfections with a frown. His requirements are not as stiff as my own.

I am bathed in a grace that covers all flaws.

"Lord, if I strive for anything," I pray, "let it be a perfect heart."

I look around me with a smile, toss the cleaning rag toward the sink, and head for the phone to call Emily.

I expect myself to be consistently witty, efficient and cellulite-free.

47

Big Britches

Kids have an annoying habit of acting like parents.

Great Leadership

In our church we have several large men on our board of deacons. One day, as I helped my 3-year-old dress, I playfully poked her protruding belly while tucking her shirt in. She proudly drew herself up, patted her tummy and pronounced, "Look, I'm a deacon!"

DEBORAH ALTSMAN, HARRISBURG, N.C.

Mama's Boy

Four-year-old Chelli thought it would be a good idea to marry the 3-year-old neighbor boy. Unfortunately, her plans hit a snag.

"That Doug!" she came home complaining. "I asked him to marry me and would you believe it? He doesn't want to leave his mama!"

MARGARET SHAUERS, GREAT BEND, KAN.

Workin' Late

For several months, my husband worked a great deal of overtime, and our 4-year-old son began to pick up his business jargon. One day I asked my son, who was busy coloring, to help his sister pick up their toys.

"Mom, I can't," he replied. "I have to work overtime with this project or else I won't be on schedule."

THERESE HALE, SAN ANGELO, TEXAS

To Have and To Hold . . . and Bite

My 6-year-old son was talking about a favorite little girl in his class. It occurred to me that he had not grasped the more delicate aspects of a loving relationship as he told me: "There's a girl in my class I'm gonna marry. I know she kicks and fights and spits, but I'm gonna marry her!"

ANN KABANUCK, SPRINGDALE, ARK.

"Honey, please tell Mommy where you transferred all of Daddy's money to."

"Aren't we getting kinda weird about the whole baby-naming thing, Beverly?"

52

"Goo Goo, Ga Ga . . ."

The real last word on babies.

by Marti Attoun

Show Time

When choosing an obstetrician, remember the important stuff.

"If the obstetrician you are considering is camera shy, drop him immediately."

Every pregnancy manual offers the same tips on choosing an obstetrician: Interview him (or her). Assess his attitudes on issues such as nutrition, weight gain, drugs during labor and the father's role in childbirth. Find someone you can communicate with and trust.

Forget it. Here's what you really need to know before you go into labor: How photogenic is the doctor? He doesn't have to look like Robert Redford, but on the other hand, you don't want a bunch of pictures of Mr. Ed in the baby book.

If the obstetrician you are considering is camera shy, drop him immediately.

As prospective parents, you'll want to find out if the doctor or his supporting cast can operate a video camera so the father can get his mug in the pictures during labor, too. Also, is the doctor a natural story teller or will he need cue cards to help fill those long gaps during filming? These productions often run to miniseries length so you need someone who is comfortable improvising scripts for 12 hours running.

You can ignore the doctor's framed credentials decorating his wall, but for heaven's sake, do not ignore his walls. Shop around until you find an obstetrician with a delivery set that you can live with. For example, my husband Otto and I chose a backdrop with pastel floral print walls that added a touch of Hollywood glamour to our production of baby Abe. Remember that you'll be seeing reruns of this movie at every family gathering for the next 10 years. Blank, white walls can get stale after awhile.

Another important consideration for us as new parents was the number of electrical outlets at the delivery scene. Otto wanted to be prepared if the battery conked on the video camera or if he needed to hook up additional lights to create special effects. For example, he did some experimenting with backlighting and ended up with a scene that Alfred Hitchcock would appreciate.

Even after all this care in selecting the obstetrician and delivery site, you'll still have surprises along the way to the recovery room. Sometimes the camera man faints or gets sick. The leading lady may try to block some of the best shots, and the dialogue of the supporting cast may be limited and repetitious—"Come on, you can do it. Come on." Even worse, the proud producer may shoot the first and only take with the lens cover on.

When this happens, though, a good obstetrician will remind you that a star was born anyway.

Free Advice . . . and Fairly Priced!

What is it about a new baby that triggers a compulsion to give advice to first-time parents?

by Sharon Hinck

And it came to pass that it was time for me to be delivered. And I brought forth my firstborn son, and wrapped him in Pampers, and laid him in a car-seat. Although we heard no angel choirs, Ted and I knew that baby Joel was very special, and our hearts were singing, "Glory to God in the highest." I never suspected what was ahead for us that first Sunday back at the church where Ted and I worked.

Joel was an adorable bundle, and people who had never given me so much as a nod stopped to gush over him. But having 400 adoptive "grandmas" to contend with was a bit overwhelming.

"Dear, are you sure he's still breathing in there?" one woman whispered, appalled at the soft front-pack carrier that held my sleepy baby.

"You shouldn't have come home from the hospital so soon. Elmer Larson's Aunt Jolene had a baby that died of jaundice when . . ."

"Ooooh! What a cute head of hair! Now you be sure to use lots of lotion on him so he doesn't get cradle cap. Cindy Wilson's little girl had hair like that and her scalp was always flaking . . ."

I smiled and nodded, dazed. My fragile bit of young-mother confidence quickly drained away. Opinions on child care were as dogmatic as they were varied. Some of the grandmas praised me for my wisdom in breast-feeding, while others worried Joel would starve if I didn't feed him cereal at two weeks of age as they had fed their babies decades ago.

I never seemed to get Joel dressed quite right. "I don't mean to criticize, but don't you think he should have a hat on today when it's so windy? I knew a boy who lost all hearing . . ."

Our church didn't believe in a church nursery ("Young children need to hear the Word!") and when Joel developed into a squirmy and very vocal church-goer, the

57

advice increased. "Sit in the front row"; "sit near the back"; "bring a bottle"; "give him Cheerios"; "give him toys to play with"; "don't give him toys, so he'll fall asleep."

I didn't hear a sermon for almost a year. Joel and I inevitably had to leave halfway through the service, to the frowns of all the grandmas whose babies had never cried in church.

What is it about a newborn baby that triggers a compulsion to give advice to the new parents? My situation may have been atypical—my being married to a full-time church worker—but I've noticed the phenomenon with other new parents, as well. Even a normally silent grocery clerk has more suggestions than Ann Landers when a baby is in range.

There are several possible explanations. Perhaps it is because new parents often look young and inexperienced— completely incapable of caring for a tiny miracle of God. I'm sure I looked awkward and insecure when juggling Joel, blankets, and an overstuffed diaper bag. I *was* awkward and insecure. Or perhaps it is because babies evoke wonderful

"Ooooh! What a cute head of hair! Now you be sure to use lots of lotion on him . . ."

memories that prompt even total strangers to relive vicariously their past experiences as parents.

Unfortunately, memories distort over the years. My own grandmother is convinced that my mom had us potty trained at six months (no way!), and she can't understand why it is taking me so long to get my children trained.

Perhaps it is caused by a normal human tendency to be "back-seat drivers." I remember smiling sagely as I watched friends who were new parents struggle with strained spinach, tantrums, and leaky diapers. With the arrogance of ignorance, I knew that, when I became a parent, I'd be able to handle those things better. I'd have a system.

Now my single friends smile sagely at me, as they watch my parenting efforts. I know what they're thinking. At least they usually have the sense to hold their tongues. They know if they make any "expert" suggestions, they'll be recruited to baby-sit.

It's encouraging to know that the flood of advice does recede in time. With a second or third child, you lose that dazed, confused look. And you're too busy to stop and listen to impractical suggestions anyway.

In fact, it won't be long before you find yourself visiting with a friend who has just become a new parent, and hear yourself saying, "Have you tried swaddling him? That always worked for me when Joel had colic . . ."

"He needs a change and a haircut."

by Marti Attoun

One Baby, Large Order of Stuff to Go

Why does a short trip with baby require 37 pounds of equipment?

You've seen those articles: "How to Visit Europe (Africa, Dallas) on Less Than Five Dollars a Day." That's not the kind of book I want to read. I'm waiting for someone to write, "How to Visit Anywhere While Hauling Less Than 50 Pounds a Day."

I'm talking about traveling with a baby. By my calculation, a short trip to the grocery store or post office with a 15-pound baby requires packing along a minimum of 37 pounds of equipment. A more adventurous trip to a shopping outlet requires at least 56 pounds of necessities. A day-long visit to a baby sitter adds another 20 pounds. An out-of-town visit isn't even worth figuring, because no one could possibly have the strength for it.

That's why I was amazed when my husband Otto suggested a spur-of-the-moment

"Just grab the baby. I'll meet you in the car," Otto hollered on his way out.

trip to a local eatery for a platter of greasy onion rings.

"Just grab the baby. I'll meet you in the car," he hollered on his way out.

I sprung open the diaper bag. Into this I pitched three diapers, a little tub of diaper wipes, changing pad, diaper rash goo, a rattle and a complete change of clothes. I waved my arm out the window to gauge the temperature and decided to throw a light blanket in the bag and a hat to cover those precious little ears.

Otto honked.

I ran to the fridge, grabbed a bottle, warmed it under hot water, then filed it in the diaper bag. Just to be safe, I tossed a can of formula and plastic bottle bags in there, along with the can opener and a bib.

Otto honked again.

I grabbed the infant seat, snatched the seat cover from the swing and put it back on the infant seat, then plopped the sleeping baby into the seat. The baby in his seat went under my left armpit, I nabbed the stroller and grabbed my purse with my teeth.

Otto pressed his entire body against the horn.

I opened the door with my toe, caught it with my rear and proceeded slowly toward the car. The baby let out a howl and I suddenly remembered . . . the pacifier. I dumped everything but the baby and ran back into the house and began a room-by-room plunder for the magic plug.

I found the pacifier, scooped up the baby in his seat, transferred the baby from his infant seat to his approved car seat, then loaded the infant seat, stroller and diaper bag into the hatch.

Finally, I settled into the car.

"You know, I'm not really hungry anymore," Otto said.

by Marti Attoun

The Truth About Baby Books

"Sorry kids. You have no past except as I remember it."

I fully intended to record the firsts, but whenever I had a spare moment, I made a clear-cut choice—snore, not record.

Some day, when my three kids start asking questions about their tothood, I hope I can find the words to tell them, "Sorry guys, but you have no history. Your mama did not keep up your baby book."

Last week, when I plundered the closet and tried to scare up a spring wardrobe, I ran across them again—the life stories of my kids. Blank. If a stranger were to look at Oscar's book, he would know that he had a footprint and colic. That's all.

Belle's book had a notation that she appeared to watch Phil Donahue when she was only three weeks old and had 13 straight hairs. Baby Abe's name wasn't even recorded on his book yet.

I had a guilt attack big enough to crease a camel.

You see, I fully intended to record their firsts, but somehow the sleepless nights slipped into diaper-changing days, and whenever I had a spare moment, I made a clear-cut choice—snore, not record.

It wouldn't be so bad if I weren't surrounded by writing mothers. My cousin Mary could put Janet Dailey to shame. She just finished her 12th novel on little Heidi.

She can tell you the hour when the kid first uttered "Mama," perched on a potty chair, gummed a teething biscuit; and where she went on her first outing, what she wore and what she weighed. She's mounted her daughter's first snips of hair, her first booties and every baby tooth that's dropped from her mouth.

Even my friend Molly, mother of three tireless tykes, has enough material for a mini-series. Not only has she filled a brag book with descriptions of the first patty-cakes, first tooth buds and first creepings, but she also has tape-recorded the first words and every holiday. For a while she kept a calendar on the trio, filling each day's blank with clever sayings and acts. And filling me with despair.

"Here. You'll want this picture to stick in Oscar's baby book," she told me not long ago when all our little ones attended a birthday party.

"Thanks," I gushed and grabbed the picture of Oscar's mug under chocolate frosting. "I hope I can find a bare page to put it on."

I mean, how could I tell this Mother Historian of the Year that I don't even have the birthdate recorded yet? And that all of the kids' pictures are tossed, undated, into a large diaper box?

I must admit that there is one benefit to having baby book writer's block. I have to rely on my own imperfect memory to supply the facts. For example, the other night a group of us were marveling at our clever cubs.

"Little Bethy sang 'Old MacDonald Had a Farm' when she was 2," Molly said smugly. "I've got her on tape. It's so cute."

"Why, my Lincoln was 18 months and knew how many sides were on a triangle," June said.

"I don't mean to brag," Marlene said, "but my Craig could say 'hello' in three foreign languages before he was 3."

"That's nothing," I said, puffing with pride. "My little Oscar could tell you the presidents of the United States when he was only 13 months old. He used to sit on the big pot and just spout them out."

"The big pot?" Molly whispered.

"Where's his baby book?" she demanded.

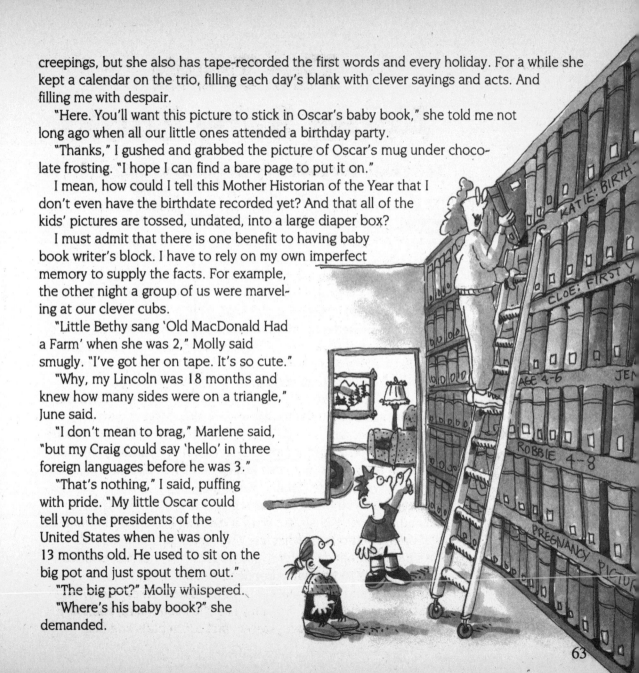

"My teacher caught me praying!"

Howard Be Thy Name

A spirited look at kids and God.

If your child wrote God a note, what would it say?

Dear God
It is great
the way
you always
get the
Stars in
the right
places.

Jeff

Dear God,
    If you watch in
Church on Sunday
I will show you
my new shoes

    Mickey D.

Dear God,
Instead of letting people die
and haveing to make new ones
why don't you just
keep the ones you got now?

Jane

Dear God,
Thank you for
the baby brother
but what I prayed
for was a Puppy

Joyce

Dear God,
Please send Denni
to a different
this year.

Peter

Did You Really Mean Do UNto
Others As They Do UNto You,
Because If You Did Then I'm
Going to Fix My Brother.

Darla

Clark
amp

Dear God

What does it mean you
are a jealous God. I
thought you had everything

Jane

Dear God —
Please put a —
nother Holiday
between Christmas
and Easter.
There is nothing good
in there now.

Ginny

Dear God,
I am doing
the best I can.

Frank

Excerpted from Children's Letters to God: The
New Collection, compiled by Stuart Hampel and
Eric Marshall and illustrated by Tom Bloom
(Workman). Used by permission.

A Man Called Howard

We were driving home from church one Sunday when our 7-year-old daughter asked, "Mom, who is Howard?"

I replied, "I don't know. Where did you hear that name?"

"In Sunday school," said my daughter. "My teacher read a verse that said, 'Our Father, who art in heaven, Howard be thy name.'"

TINA LAUBSCHER, CHATTANOOGA, TENN.

On the Tip of His Tongue

My son's kindergarten Sunday school class was singing "Jesus Loves Me," when Tommy excitedly announced he had a tape at home which had two verses to that song on it.

The teacher asked him if he'd like to sing the other verse for the class so they could all learn it.

Tommy thought a moment. "Well, I don't remember the words," he finally said. "But I could hum it!" he cheerfully added.

LORI BORGER, POWAY, CALIF.

Answered Prayer

One rainy summer morning I looked out my kitchen window to find my son Derek standing in the backyard crying. I went out and asked what was wrong. Between sobs he blurted out, "Yesterday it was so hot, I prayed to Jesus for rain. Then Daddy came home last night and told me we could go water skiing today. Now it's raining and we can't go and it's all my fault—I forgot to tell Jesus I changed my mind."

LAURA ABBOTT, HAMPDEN, MASS.

Gentle Reminder

I have discovered that if I don't have my quiet time every morning, I tend to be grouchy and lose my temper over the most insignificant things.

Recently, my 4-year-old son, Andrew, reminded me of this need for daily prayer. He had innocently made a mistake and spilled something, and I immediately went into a screaming tirade.

Andrew ended my tantrum when he quietly asked, "Mommy, you forgot to ask Jesus to help you be nice today, didn't you?"

CATHY FUSSELL, APOPKA, FLA.

Prehistoric Appetizer

As I was cleaning my 3-and-a-half-year-old son Christopher's room, I overheard him say, "Dear God, thank you for this food. Amen." Turning to see why he was saying grace as he played, I saw his Hulk Hogan doll surrounded by his toy dinosaurs. He looked up and said, "They're going to eat him."

TRACY SMITH, CANON CITY, COLO.

Missed Lines

My 3-year-old son was watching me stumble through aerobics in our living room. I was attempting to get back into shape after the birth of our youngest child.

Suddenly he shouted his new memory verse to me: "Joshua 1, verse 9. Have I not commanded you? Be strong and curvaceous!"

SARAH LIMA, MILTON, WIS.

Preacher Leash

During a service in our church, an evangelist ran to the edge of the platform with his microphone cord dragging behind. Leaning out toward the congregation, he waved his fist to loudly emphasize a point.

A frightened little girl in the third row leaned over to her mother and asked, "Mommy, if he gets loose, will he hurt us?"

TERRY W. GREEN, FORT WORTH, TEXAS

"Proper English is, 'I saw the door,' not 'I sawed the door.'"

Dad Gum It!

Chewing the fat with fathers.

by Marti Attoun

Otto's Big Day

Shopping for Father's Day really ought to be a snap.

I have never had to bother reading those clever gift guides for the man who has everything. I've just spent two weeks hunting for the perfect Father's Day gift for the man who has nothing.

It sounds simple, but it isn't. Do the kids and I buy Otto a new shirt, tie, weedwhacker, gasoline can, tennis racket or watch?

Heavens, no. All Otto wants for Father's Day is a $42 octopus for his aquarium. I figure it would have a lifespan of about 15 minutes at our house—just long enough to seep through the crack in the lid and embrace my mother during her daily visit.

You'd think it'd

> **"Heavens! All Otto wants for Father's Day is a $42 octopus for his aquarium."**

be a snap shopping for a man whose eyeglasses are held together with rubber cement and prayer, but it isn't. Otto disdains the purchase of anything practical.

"Don't get any funny ideas about buying me clothes for Father's Day," he warned me the other evening. "A person can only wear one outfit at a time, so why buy a bunch of stuff to decorate the closet?"

At the time he was wearing one of my stretched-out T-shirts—the one that says "The Best Man For The Job May Be A Woman."

"You really need a new suit, Otto, for your next formal affair," I strongly suggested. At the last company party, Otto received his 10-year-pin just in time. He used it to keep his pants together the rest of the evening.

"That little rip can be fixed," he informed me. "My Dad paid good money for that suit. I was the best-dressed guy at the senior prom."

You'd think it'd be a breeze buying a Father's Day gift for a man who packs in trash bags and orange crates on family vacations and occasional business trips. But it isn't.

"Don't you dare buy me any luggage, either," Otto forewarned. "For the price of luggage I could fill those fish tanks with six huma huma triggerfishes and a dozen yellow tangs. Besides, trash bags are more versatile than suitcases. You can squish them around the spare tire and use them for ponchos if you get caught in a down-pour."

"What about a new rear view mirror for your truck, then?" I sighed. "Now that's something you really can't live without." A neighborhood bully recently removed ours.

"Definitely a luxury," Otto said and swiveled his head five times before I ordered him to stop.

"New shoes, Otto?" I asked, and pointed to his scruffy footwear.

"Nah. I'm going to get these retreaded, and they'll be good for another 10,000 miles," he said smugly.

On Father's Day, the man who has nothing still does.

ONE "BIGG" HAPPY FAMILY by Wheeler

IT SAYS HERE THERE ARE MANY THINGS YOU CAN DO TO PREVENT CATCHING YOUR CHILD'S COLD.

SNIFF

OF MOST IMPORTANCE IS TO WASH YOUR HANDS EVERY TIME YOU WIPE THEIR NOSE.

BLOW!

HONK!

RIGHT, BIG GUY?

SNIFF

AH-CHOO!

77

Dad's Dictionary of Household Words

An examination has revealed that certain commonly accepted definitions are . . . way off.

by Dave Branon

Dictionaries distort. They often don't tell us what words really mean.

Did you ever look up the word "nap," for instance? My dictionary says "nap" means, "to doze or sleep lightly for a short time." Ha! Obviously spoken by a non-dad. It ought to read, "A state of war between parent and a young child, whereby the child is, after the better part of the afternoon, subdued to a state of temporary isolation that is immediately broken by the voice of a sibling who arrives home from school shouting, 'What's to eat?!'" Now there's a definition a parent can understand.

So, in an effort to update the language, we present a short glossary of household terms along with definitions the dictionaries were afraid to print.

Baby sitter: Nearly extinct breed of human. Those who do exist either live on the other side of town or have something else to do next Friday.

Boy: Young male of the human species. In early years is known for unusual feeding habits. Likes to see how far food can travel, rather than how good it tastes. Before the age of 3, often is employed as a product tester to see: (a) how long French-style green beans can remain suspended from the dining room ceiling; (b) how long Dad's ears can endure hearing the TV at full volume; and (c) how long a human infant can survive while trapped between a sliding glass door and a screen door. Has been known to scale tall refrigerators with no ropes.

Checkbook: Essential part of a dad's survival kit. This coupon book gives parents two days (three over weekends) to figure out where they are going to get some money before the bank starts foreclosure proceedings.

Crisis: Synonym for parenthood. A phenomenon that never affects children—

even when there are only five minutes until church starts and they haven't started getting dressed yet. This word is unknown to 2-year-old boys, who don't even care whether the medical center is open as they stand precariously on the back edge of the couch while holding a sharp object.

Done: A term that is used only after the word "never." It usually refers to some form of work or project, as in "The yardwork is never done."

Free time: Archaic term denoting a mysterious time period experienced only by college students and striking football players. Any dad who attempts to have free time will instantly begin to hear strange sounds—phones ringing, children throwing up and dogs whining to go for a walk.

"Good night": Magical code word. Transforms tired children into thirsty, sick-to-their-stomach, talkative, frightened gremlins. These gremlins turn into sleeping children after (a) three threats upon their life, (b) two drinks of water, (c) one night-light, (d) one bedtime story after another, (e) 35 minutes or (f) all of the above.

Grocery store: A greedy, bottomless pit of a place where parents congregate daily to redistribute their wealth.

Hurry: Something 12-year-old girls are in when their parents aren't, and aren't in when their parents are.

Keys: Designed by the same people who brought us the Stealth bomber. They are made of a substance that renders them invisible to the human eye until two hours after they are needed. They often reside in openings in couches and in unused coat pockets.

Money: A fast-moving, slippery substance that seems to gravitate toward grocery stores.

Newspaper: A mass of recyclables that arrives at your doorstep (or in the shrubs or on the roof) daily. This mass lies dormant in the family room for two days before being deposited in the corner of the garage, where it remains until someone from the school paper drive comes to haul it away. It's been reported that a newspaper actually has been picked up and read by a parent. This has yet to be verified.

No: 1. Maybe 2. Go check with Mom 3. Yes.

Normalcy: A state of affairs that has been known to exist next door but never at your house.

Panic: The feeling of fear that overcomes parents of a hungry toddler when they discover that one of the refrigerator magnets is missing.

Parenthood: A condition of perpetual motion in which an adult is forced into voluntary action. This person takes on a number of mysterious functions, such as referee, taxi driver, plumber, waste disposal manager, pastor, athletic coach, math expert, maid, time management supervisor, cook and bicycle repair person.

Piano lessons: Something dads hate to pay for so their kids can hate to go to them so they can come home and hate to practice.

Professional photographer: A man or woman who takes your money and then

proceeds to make your children cry, spit up, and frown. Noted for ability to say "boo" and shake stuffed bunnies at children who don't like to be scared or see quick movement. Also adept at assessing that children are "just having a bad day."

Relaxation: The fleeting calm you feel during the five minutes it takes to drive from where you dropped off child A to where you have to pick up child B.

Sack of groceries: Half a week's pay.

Serviceman: A person you pay to come into your house to insult you in front of the children. Favorite lines of a serviceman are, "Why didn't you try plugging the TV in?" and "All I had to do, sir, was light the pilot light."

Telephone: A usually harmless device whose ringing sound signals children to begin talking loudly, fighting, pouring sugar all over the kitchen floor and turning up the volume on the TV.

Used by parents to test hearing in one ear while the other is subjected to high-decibel noises.

"Time for bed": A code phrase that causes sixth-graders to remember that they forgot to do their math homework. (See "Good night.")

ONE "BIGG" HAPPY FAMILY by Wheeler

Profound Declaration of the Obvious

My hobby is woodworking. I often make toys for our three children or furniture for our home. One evening I was diligently working on a project in my basement workshop. Upstairs my wife raised her voice above the loud sounds of my power tools to ask our 2-year-old, "What is Daddy making?"

With a look of annoyance, he replied, "Noise!"

STEPHEN STORMS, BUSHNELL, ILL.

Prompt Love

One afternoon my 2-year-old son came bursting into the kitchen telling me he had a hug and a kiss for me. As I knelt down, he threw his arms around me and said, "I love you, Mama." I tried to hold him and savor the moment, but he dashed out again. Tears of joy welled from my eyes as I thought of the wonderful rewards of parenting. Then I heard him call, "I did it, Daddy!"

BETH BAEFIELD, APEX, N.C.

Outnumbere

What happens to the typical American male when he gets three daughters—and no sons? When even the family dog is female? And Mom is gone for the weekend?

by Mark A. Tabb

Typical American male—that's me. If there is a sporting event on TV I watch it. Baseball, basketball, football, even golf. I like watching people do things I could never do and make them appear simple. I get a thrill out of catching fish. Never mind that the net cost comes out to $27.96 per pound by the time you figure in the price of equipment and licenses. It doesn't matter.

I always believed a son would make all of the above better. We would be a team. Inseparable. A dynamic duo. Being a typical American male, I would also be a typical overanxious father. There would be a baseball glove in the hospital crib. I would introduce my son to doubleheaders and slam dunks as early in life as possible. We would share it all.

I tried to convince my wife, Valerie, that we should name our future son after the 1977 New York Yankees' outfield—Lou Pinella, Mickey Rivers and Reggie Jackson. When she pointed out that our child would have to live with the name Louis Michael Reginald Tabb for the rest of his life, we decided to look somewhere other than the sports page for the perfect name.

We settled on Caleb Andrew after the Old Testament spy who stood against the crowd and the disciple who brought his brother to Jesus.

But the doctor delivered our first child and asked us, "What are you going to name Caleb's sister?" And Bethany Rachel looked up at me with her big, dark eyes. *Who needs a boy when you can have a girl?* The room seemed to get a little foggy.

To celebrate Bethany's second day in the world we watched a baseball game on TV together. The New York Yankees were playing the California Angels. I pointed out to her that just because one team was named after heavenly messengers we did not have to root for them.

As I recall, her reaction to baseball was much like her mother's—she slept through most of it.

Two years later, Bethany and I spent our evenings getting acquainted with Hannah Michelle while she was still inside my wife's body.

When Hannah was born, she found the world a rather annoying place to be. So she did what any rational person would do—she cried. I placed my hand on her back as she lay under the warming light and spoke to her as I had before she was born. She suddenly stopped crying and laid very still as though she felt secure and safe.

So I did what any rational dad would do. I cried.

Sarah Elizabeth came into this world two years after Hannah and staked a claim on my left shoulder for a sleeping place.

Night after night, Valerie handed our

third daughter over to me for the magic shoulder treatment. Sarah liked it there so much that she'd wake up when I put her down.

Now I'm the only male in an all-female household. Every stuffed animal in our house has been given a distinctively feminine name. Even our dog is female. Our tomcat couldn't take the pressure and ran away.

A typical

American male must make adjustments to survive in an all-female family. Barbies and paper dolls replace Los Angeles Lakers paraphernalia. Adjustment time comes when Hannah, with eyes that would have melted Stalin's heart, says, "Daddy, will you play Barbies with me?" In the male-dominated neighborhood where I grew up, we had no tolerance for boys who played with any doll that wasn't a G.I. Joe. But I say to Hannah, "Of course, Sweetheart, I'll play Barbies with you." I'm thankful that Barbie now has Ferraris and Jeeps to cruise around in. That's my job—Official Barbie Car Driver.

All three girls came with curly hair as standard equipment. Long, flowing curls are a beautiful sight for a dad to behold—until Mom goes out of town for the weekend. "Honey, you'll be fine with the girls by yourself. It will be good for the four of you to spend some time alone together."

It *was* good, until Sunday

I'm the only male in an all-female household. Every stuffed animal in our house has been given a distinctively feminine name.

morning—the one day of the weekend when they actually had to look presentable in public.

Dresses were no problem. Bethany and Hannah could pick out what they wanted to wear. Sarah, like most 2-year-olds, will wear whatever you talk her into. Even finding three pairs of matching socks was less taxing than I had anticipated (I had expected something just short of the search for the Ark of the Covenant).

There they were—bodies bathed, teeth brushed, clothes on. Only one thing left.

Few things cause a man to admit that he is helpless and frightened. Empires have been attacked with more resolve than I had as I approached the hairbrush.

I had one thing going for me: as pastor of the church no one would say anything too critical of the girls' appearance for fear of becoming a sermon illustration. I took full advantage of this knowledge, more out of necessity than desire to put fear in the hearts of my congregation. They seemed to find my daugh-

ters presentable, even if not as stylish as when Mommy was around.

In addition to inviting me into their world, my girls share mine as well. All three have declared themselves public enemies of the local bluegill population. While stalking this elusive fish, Bethany and Hannah conduct scientific research into earthworm durability. Actually, they don't experiment on the worms as much as try to domesticate them.

Televised sports remain part of our world as well. My girls have learned the essentials: how to cheer and how to boo. Hannah is especially fond of Michael Jordan. She pretends she is "like Mike"—sticking her tongue out to one side. A Michael poster hovers over her ballerina and Little Mermaid posters. Bethany and I almost drove Hannah to tears during the 1992 NBA finals as we screamed, "Glide, Clyde, glide!" at Clyde Drexler of the Portland Trail Blazers. Hannah thought it unfair to cheer for anyone but Michael.

My daughters also try to watch football with me. They understand that there is some team from Dallas, where Bethany was born, that we are supposed to cheer for. And there is a team from Washington that we are supposed to root against. Things become complicated when they ask, "Which team is Michael Jordan's?"

I am outnumbered but overjoyed. Daughters and fathers have the potential to have one of the most unique of all human relationships—and I get to experience it three times over.

I am outnumbered but overjoyed. Daughters and fathers have the potential to have one of the most unique of all human relationships—and I get to experience it three times over.

Long ago I was told to enjoy my children while they were young. I've listened. Right now my girls think Daddy is the greatest man on the earth.

I realize time will change this. As they grow up, other men will come into their lives. One day, each daughter will believe there is another man more wonderful than her father. I'll have to learn to call those men sons.

But whatever the future may hold, I know this: Bethany, Hannah and Sarah will always be my little girls. They'll never get so big they can't wrap their arms around my neck, look into my eyes and say, "I love you, Daddy." And there will never come a day when I will not love them with all my heart.

"You're eating Billy's science project."

The Class Menagerie

A short walk on the wild side of school.

That Walter!

In every class there's a Walter—perfectly behaved, perfectly brilliant. And some other mother is always beaming.

by Joan Wester Anderson

After years of serving as a helper at the parish pre-school, I've reached an inescapable conclusion: Every class has a Wonderful Walter.

Wonderful Walters come in all sizes, shapes and colors. Their prime function is to be paragons of Christian goodness at all times, thus humiliating mothers who previously had assumed their own children were doing splendidly in the virtue and talent departments.

Nothing bruises a mother's ego more than watching a 4-year-old paint in oils while her own tot struggles to figure out the difference between red and blue.

When I met the current Walter, I recognized him immediately. He was carefully picking lint off his coat and cap before arranging them on a wooden hanger. My daughter tossed her jacket into the nearest pile of slush and headed for the toy corner, perfectly comfortable amid clutter and screams.

While the teacher and I cut construction paper shapes for the day's craft, the children played, painted, and chattered over the strains of a Winnie the Pooh record. Walter created a map of North America, complete with mountain ranges and state capitals, and then replaced Winnie with a

Grieg concerto from his collection.

"That Walter!" the teacher murmured affectionately. "He certainly adds a touch of class, doesn't he?"

We were interrupted by shrieking from the toy corner where my daughter and a playmate were engaged in a tug of war over a teddy bear. "Mine! Mine!" screamed my adorable one.

Deftly, Walter separated the girls while giving them a lecture on the merits of sisterly love, then quickly mended Teddy's leg. "That Walter!" the teacher smiled again.

The group cut, crayoned and

91

glued their way through the day's craft, a picture of a sailboat. Several boys ate their crayons, and my daughter dumped her paste pot over the head of a neighbor. Walter remained clean and unruffled, producing a perfect replica of John Paul Jones.

While the class listened to a Bible story, I hosed down the tables, then set out crackers and juice.

"Snack time!" I announced brightly, forgetting to dodge the stampede. It was Walter who helped me to my feet, pulled out my chair and poured me another cup of juice.

The rest of the morning passed in a blur. During Show and Tell, Walter treated the children to his butterfly collection. My daughter held up my checkbook.

During cleanup time, Walter swept the floor and spray-polished the sink tiles while I tried to persuade the rest of the group to toss a few blocks in the bin.

Mercifully, the morning ended. As I grimly stuffed my daughter into her jacket and hat, I felt a tug on my sleeve. It was Walter, looking up at me from under his incredibly long lashes.

"I have a slight problem," he confided.

"Really? Did the stock market take a tumble?"

"No. I can't get my mitten off and I—I need to suck my thumb."

My heart soared.

My daughter had broken her thumb-sucking habit months ago. "Oh, Walter!" I grinned, throwing my arms around him. "I absolutely love you!"

"Actually," Walter told me, "it's nothing to get emotional about."

The teacher smiled fondly. "That Walter!" she chuckled.

I couldn't have put it any better.

For Show and Tell, Walter brought his butterfly collection. My daughter held up my checkbook.

Unexpected Demotion

When my son was preparing for "career week" at his elementary school, we discussed my job as an airline customer-services representative. I mentioned that one of my responsibilities was to load passengers' luggage at the check-in counter. Later, I learned that my son had listed my occupation as "Bag Lady."

ERIKA JOINER, SACRAMENTO, CALIF.

Canceled Cleanliness

During the school year my teenage son arises extra early so he can take a bath before breakfast. One icy morning this past winter, while he was bathing, I turned on the television set to hear the announcement that school had been called off. I thought he would be happy, but I was surprised when he said disgustedly, "You mean, I took a bath for nothing?"

DIANA WEST, JOPLIN, MO.

Canine Kid

My daughter's greatest joy in first grade was bringing the most astounding Show and Tell item.

One day when we were running late she grabbed something for Show and Tell—I decided to give her a chance to decide on her own what to take.

When she got home from school that day, she informed me that she had eaten the entire dog biscuit in front of her class. But her real sense of accomplishment came the next day when another little girl brought a cat treat and couldn't eat the whole thing.

DEBORAH CLIMER, SALEM, ORE.

"I'm telling you, Mom, she said we were going to practice *cursing* writing tomorrow!"

Alphabet Zoup

A mouthful on kidspeak.

"How High Is the Sky?"

(Inquiring Short People Want to Know)

by Joan Wester Anderson

Memories of my wedding day are a bit hazy. I recall vowing to "love, honor and cherish," but nowhere was there mentioned another obligation—to have all the answers. I have since discovered, however, that this is a parent's primary obligation. Providing love, food, shelter, Sunday school, orthodontia and piano lessons pales in significance to the ultimate responsibility: Know Everything.

It starts slowly and in rather precious fashion as the preschooler lisps, "How high is the sky, Daddy?" "How old is God?" It's fun at that stage to think of whimsical answers. One cannot help but enjoy the unaccustomed role of oracle.

But the worm soon turns. "Where did I come from, Mommy?" can sometimes be sidetracked with: "Cleveland, honey. Have a cookie." But not if it is asked in a crowded elevator, as it most likely will be.

Other queries inevitably raised in public include: "Why is that lady so fat?" and "How come you and Daddy were yelling this morning?" When confronted with such brainteasers, a wise parent simply stares straight ahead, pretending that the child belongs to someone else.

As kids grow, they develop favorite questions, and ask them with astounding regularity. One of the most common is, "Mom, where's my _____?" (Fill in the blank.)

Although she did not major in inventory control, Mother is presumed to possess a photographic memory, instantly knowing the whereabouts of a pair of doll shoes, a safety pin, a red pencil, or the peanut butter sandwich left on the bureau last Wednesday. Smart mothers turn the tables and ask a few questions of their own: "Did you look in the piano bench? In the potted fern? Under the radiator?" Having thus done their duties, moms are free to return to their magazines and bonbons.

Another favorite query at our house is "What's for dinner?" Each child regards it his or her solemn obligation to inquire thus at three-minute intervals each evening. Since we have five children, dinner is usually late because I am so busy answering questions. To stem the tide, I once posted the menu on our kitchen blackboard. As the first son

began the nightly ritual, I wordlessly pointed east.

"Why are you pointing?" he asked. "And what's for dinner?"

"Read the menu," I answered.

"How come we're having a menu, Mom? How come?"

"READ IT!"

"S-P-A . . ." he began. "Let's see . . . spumoni? Split pea? Mom, what does S-P-A . . ?

"Spaghetti!"

"Oh. You aren't putting those yucky tomato things in the sauce, are you? And are we having salad, too? Do I have to eat salad, Mom? Huh, Mom?"

Another child rushes in. "Hi, Mom. What's for dinner?"

I didn't have any spaghetti that night, as I was busy burning the blackboard.

My husband has learned to cope with the kinds of questions that have no answer, such as, "Dad, what would you do if you had all the money in the world?" or "Who's better—boys or girls?" He simply replies, "Go ask your mother."

But neither of us knows how to recognize the significant question, the one that is sometimes buried among the trivia. "What would happen," my young daughter once asked, "If I stuffed clay down the toilet?"

"What do you think?" I cleverly parried.

"I think you better come and look."

By the time our kids reach pre-adolescence, we can expect a breather, because a child of that age regards parents as leftovers from the Dark Ages, and wouldn't dream of seeking our opinions on any subject. But the questions soon begin again. And a taste of "Why can't I spend $150 on a pair of jeans—I earned it!" "Can I have the car tonight?" and "Why is the grass green?"

Somehow, we manage. Ill-equipped, lacking the wisdom of age or doctorate in child psychology, we become what God has always intended parents to be—a child's first font of knowledge. We do not always realize, as we answer a toddler's questions with patience, that we are paving the way for a time when toddler becomes teen, and can still approach us with confidence. We do not always see that each question, however innocent, exposes our feelings, values and ideals, and gives us a chance to light the world through the coming generation.

And we don't always realize that someday the seekers will be gone. Then, amidst the welcome peace, we will catch ourselves listening for the small trusting voice that asks, "Why do mommies and daddies know so much?"

Your first obligation as a parent is to know everything.

Canada Speak

My sister, her young son Billy and his pal Kevin were having lunch at my house one day when I was surprised by a visit from a friend from Saskatchewan, Canada. I called Billy and Kevin to help carry in some of her things, and I noticed them studying her car's license plates.

"Where do you live, Ma'am?" Billy inquired.

"I'm from Saskatoon, Saskatchewan," my friend replied.

"Gee," Billy whispered to Kevin on our way back to the house, "she doesn't even speak English."

JULIANA LEWIS, EL PASO, TEXAS

Mixed Melody

My 4½-year-old, Emily, loves to sing while she is playing. Sometimes, though, she gets her words mixed up. One afternoon she sang, "Jesus loves me, this I know . . . EE-I-EE-I-O!"

MRS. E. NORRIS, ELKTON, FLA.

Deep Theology

During a heart-to-heart discussion, Dad asked, "Have you ever heard of hell?"

Five-year-old Andy thought for a moment, then said, "No, but I've heard of heck!"

BONNY L. BOYAN, PULLMAN, WASH.

Run That by Me Again?

My son Jamie was meeting the son of our new Japanese neighbors for the first time.

"It's nice to have you next door," Jamie began. "Ah . . . I don't believe I know your name."

"You know," his new friend said softly.

"No, I'm sorry, I don't know. Or at least I don't remember. Please tell me."

"You know," the boy repeated, a bit louder.

Seeing the potential misunderstanding developing between them, Jamie asked, "Well, could you spell it then, just to make sure I get it right?"

"Sure," the boy replied. "U-n-o. Uno."

GARY SEVERSON, EVERSON, WASH.

Just Following Orders

Before a nap, my husband asked our 4-year-old son, Casey, to wake him up as soon as the radio alarm went off. Waking up quite late to a blaring radio, Dad asked, "Why didn't you wake me up?"

Casey said, "You said to wake you up when the radio went off!"

BONNY L. BOYAN, PULLMAN, WASH.

100

Alphabet Zoup

My husband's younger brother had a report to do on Noah's Ark. When he went to use the encyclopedia he asked his mom, "Do I look up 'N' for Noah or 'Z' for Zark?"

MARY JANE MERREN, CLINTON, MICH.

In a Hurry

Vocabulary study is a part of the 5th-grade curriculum at our local elementary school, and from time to time the children are given lists of words that are unfamiliar to most 5th-graders. On those occasions, the teacher instructs them to look in the dictionary for the meanings of the words, then use them correctly in original sentences.

One such list included the word "homogeneous." One boy, as he hurried through the assignment, glanced only at the first definition given, "uniform." When called upon for his sentence, the student responded in a clear confident voice, "Every soldier should keep his homogeneous clean."

BETTY L. HERRING, MIDLAND, MICH.

"Don't bite it. I have to check Daddy next."

Pet Peeves

Cow say "Mooo!" Puppy say "Woof!" Mama say "No No No!"

Puppies by the Piece

One day my sister, 7-year-old niece and I went to a pet store to buy my niece a puppy. In as grown-up a voice as she could muster, she asked the owner how much they cost. "About $50 apiece," he replied.

Rather puzzled, she asked, "Well, how much does a whole one cost?"

SUZAN L. WIENER, SPRING HILL, FLA.

Barnyard Babble

My 1½-year-old daughter loves to make animal sounds. One day I heard her in her room, reciting the ones she knew: "Sheep say Baaa! Cow say Mooo! Puppy say Woof! Mama say No, no, no!"

CHERY WEBSTER, AMARILLO, TEXAS

Kitty Burnout

Our 5-year-old son Michael wants a cat but my husband, Mike, is allergic to them. One evening at Grampa's, Michael spotted his cat and said, "Daddy, I'd like a gray cat like that one."

"We can't have a cat because they make my eyes burn," Mike said.

"Well, Daddy, just don't look at it!"

ANNE GAGLIANO, MARYSVILLE, WASH.

Painful Operation

I told my 4-year-old that his grandmother had cataract surgery and we were going to visit her. When he saw the patch over her eye he said, "So that's where the cat attacked you."

HOLLY DEVINE, MATTHEWS, N.C.

Cat Got Your Tongue

Watching a nature show, my 4-year-old exclaimed, "Look—there's a wion!"

"Yes, that's a lion," I said, with a lot of emphasis on the L.

He tried again, "Wion."

"No. Lion."

"Mom, I think that's a tiger."

TONJA WELLS, N. RICHLAND HILLS, TEXAS

Four-Legged Friends

When my daughter, Valerie, was very small, there were no children her age in the neighborhood to play with. I wasn't concerned, however, because she played so well by herself and with our two dogs. When she was about 2½ the following incident occurred, which made me reconsider her need for playmates:

She was playing in the yard with the dogs when I heard a loud commotion. I ran to the door and asked Valerie what was going on.

"Oh, we were just barking at the mailman," she said.

NANCY LORD, MIDLAND, TEXAS

106

Bugsicle

As my 2-year-old son and I were playing outside, a bug landed on his arm and frightened him. I said, "Flick it off!" He proceeded to lick off the bug instead.

BARBARA CROSBY, EIGHT MILE, ALA.

Hot Sunday School Lesson

While getting my 4-year-old ready for bed one night, I asked him what he had learned at church that day. He said the teacher had told a story about three men who were thrown into a fiery furnace—"Shadrach, Meshach and A-billy-goat."

CARLA JOHNSON, BECKLEY, W. VA.

"I think we owe the children an apology."

Rules of the Roost

Lay down the law—hear the kids cackle.

What Grows Up Oft Falls Down

by Sally Wilkins

Every family is different, it's true. But science has determined that there are some universal truths parents can count on. Here are a dozen laws of life with children.

Laws of Progression

1. Resilience is a factor of birth order. First children are fragile, sensitive to a variety of foods, and awakened by loud noises. Third children are unbreakable, eat everything and could sleep through the arrival of the 9:40 Concorde.

2. Toys expand to fill the space available. And they lurk in the attic long after their proper owners have moved on to apartments of their own, which are too small to store all those boxes.

3. Nothing is ever as simple as it looks before you begin. Nor is it as complicated as it feels halfway through.

4. The older you get, the less you know. From birth to 18 months, you remember every detail of your child's birth and development. By the time he's 2, you realize you're losing it, but he thinks you know everything. From ages 6 to 12 your expertise erodes, and by the time he's 13 he knows you know nothing at all.

Laws of Inverse and Direct Proportions

5. The more help children offer, the less work they will actually do. This is not a new phenomenon. Jesus described it in His parable of two sons who went to work in the vineyard (Matt. 21:28-32).

6. The younger the child, the more stuff that goes with him. A weekend at Grandma's with a baby requires a station wagon. Nineteen years later the same child can go to Europe for the summer with a knapsack.

Law #9:
No matter how many toys, games and educational activities you provide, there's never anything to do.
(Unless it's bedtime.)

7. The more interesting the subject, the lower the audible decibel level. A child who responds "What?" when told directly to pick up her socks, can hear the words "ice cream" whispered at the opposite end of the house.

8. Quality of behavior is directly proportional to the distance of the relationship between child and adult. The most troublesome child can be expected to play nicely, make polite conversation, pick up cheerfully and volunteer to do the dishes—at a friend's house.

Laws of (No) Matter

10. No matter how much you just spent on groceries, there is never anything to eat. Unless you were saving it for tomorrow's church supper.

11. No matter how complete the explanation or how detailed the rationale, when you've finished your child will still ask "Why?"

12. No matter how much you tear your hair, wring your hands, and pound your head now, someday you will look back fondly, and say, "Remember when?"

Rub-a-Dub, Dub, Mom's In the Tub

...But not for long. Something's bound to go wrong.

by Nancy Kennedy

My life is filled with great challenges: Keeping my marriage together. Raising happy kids. Getting rid of soap scum.

But the greatest challenge so far has to be getting my kids out of the bathroom so I can get in—and then once I'm in, keeping them out.

I don't ask for much. All I want is a little privacy when I'm in the bathroom. I'd like my favorite hairbrush not to be used on the dog or tucked away in someone's lunchbox that's been left at school. Call me a nitpicker, but I don't like my eyeliner pencils used for homework or my nail file used to sharpen popsicle sticks into spears. When I reach for

GOOD 'OL MOM

G.I. JERRY

LAURA'S RUBBER DUCKIE

a washcloth, I'd prefer one that hasn't already been used to wipe out the fish tank. Just once, when blow-drying my hair, I'd like to see only one face in the mirror—mine.

And a bath. Twenty minutes of solitude for a hot, steamy bath isn't asking for much —unless you have three children like I do.

What is it about children and bathrooms? Whenever I see the door closed longer than five minutes I get suspicious— especially with my 4-year-old.

"Laura, what are you doing in there?"

"Nothing."

"Can you unlock the door so Mommy can see?"

MIKE'S ICKY 'XPERIMENT

ALISON DID IT!

MICHAEL'S HI TOPS

ALISON'S SOCKS

"Not yet. I'm busy."

"What are you busy doing?"

"Nothing."

In the past, I've discovered "nothing" to be: two dozen unwrapped bars of soap, an entire roll of toilet paper unrolled into a heap on the floor, Vaseline smeared on the mirror, and a teddy bear taking a bubble bath in the toilet.

Those things I can live with. It's the combined sounds of flushing and giggling

"I took a bath once. That was before the Great Raspberry Jello Experiment."

that cause me to panic. Echoes of "Mommy, look at my shoe spin!" and "Bye-bye toothbrush!" haunt me. The plumber, however, thinks it's cute. At $52.50 an hour, he can afford to.

The 4-year-old is nothing compared to my son. Michael is 8. An 8-year-old boy doing "nothing" in the bathroom is lying.

"Michael, what are you doing in there?"

"Nothing."

"Why is the water running?"

"What water?"

"Michael, open the door."

"Mom—I'm in the bathroom! Can't a guy have any privacy around here?"

Privacy doesn't come without a price to the mother of an 8-year-old boy. There's $2.39 to replace the tube of toothpaste that he poked hundreds of pinholes in and then squeezed to see how "cool" it looked; $1.99 for a new bent-handled extra-soft bristled toothbrush (he used mine to put shoe polish on his face—he wanted to see what he'd look like with a beard and mustache); and $32.99 to replace the electric razor. ("But Mom, didn't you ever want to see what a tennis ball looks like after being shaved?")

At least he doesn't spend nearly every waking moment in the bathroom like my 13-year-old daughter. When a teenage girl says she's doing "nothing" in the bathroom, she's doing exactly that—and it takes her an hour and a half to do it. Every hair must be in place, every blemish on the face must be inspected (and cried over). Prayers must be offered up over a too-flat chest and too-wide hips.

"Alison, what are you doing in there?"

"Nothing! Can't everybody leave me alone! Why are you always picking on me?"

"Alison, open the door."

"I'm too ugly and I'm never coming out!"

I believe her, too.

I took a bath once. January 13, 1973. That was before Magic Color-Change Donald Duck and Scrub-A-Dub Mickey took over and made the bathtub their permanent home; before the invasion of my son's Helicopter Attack Cruiser, He-Man Astrosub, and a half-dozen G.I. Joe action figures; before the Great Raspberry Jello experiment; before the bathtub ring, and mildew on the ceiling.

Oh, I've tried taking a bath since then, but I've never succeeded. There seems to be a direct relationship between my foot hitting the water and a catastrophe on the other side of the bathroom door.

One day I announced: "I'm going to take a bath. All by myself. Alone." No sooner did I put my foot in the water when I heard a tiny knock and the words, "Mommy, I have to go potty."

Three minutes later another knock. "Mom, you said you'd hem my skirt. Can you do it now?"

Another knock. "Mom, what are you doing in there?"

"Nothing. Go away."

They won't go away. I tried putting a Do Not Disturb sign on the door. They disturbed me. I locked the door. My 4-year-old picked the lock. The last time I tried to take a bath, I really thought I'd made it. I got as far as getting both feet in the tub when I heard a commotion outside the door.

"You ask her."

"Not me. You did it."

"Okay, we'll both ask. Uh, Mom, how do

you put out a fire?"

Last week, in a moment of desperation, I snatched the emergency money out of its envelope and checked into a motel. I felt adventurous and daring, and a bit naughty. A real bath—all by myself. My heart pounded in anticipation of fragrant, silky bubbles, my head resting luxuriously on a cushion, the water a comfortable 97 degrees. Then the phone rang.

"Hello, Ma'am. Sorry to disturb you, but motel maintenance will have the water shut off for a few hours."

Thirty-five dollars and my dream bath down the drain.

When I got home, I marched into the bathroom only to find towels strewn everywhere, toothpaste all over the sink, the dog licking the soap dish, Rubber Duckie bobbing in the toilet, a pile of sand on the floor, and something brown smeared on the wall.

I decided I didn't want to know what it was or how it got there—or why.

My husband found me hunched in a corner, rocking back and forth singing, "Rubber Duckie, you're the one . . ."

I had lost all semblance of sanity.

"Honey," he said, lifting me to my feet, "why don't you take a nice bath?"

A Kid's Undercover Guide to Bedtime Battles

(Maybe you need a refresher on what the other side is thinking...)

by Darleen Hainline

The battle of bedtime has plagued parents since time began. Skirmish lines are drawn from the time we take our kids home from the hospital until we send them (and our money) off to college. Goals and techniques may differ with age and experience, but all kids have meticulously honed bed-avoidance skills. Some are able to snatch an extra ten minutes by delaying bedtime. Others gauge success by the number of trips out of bed to Mom or Dad on any given night. Still others believe the prize goes to the one who crawls out of Mom and Dad's bed in the morning. Whatever the age or skill mastery, the same goal exists: Avoid that bed!

What are the basic tenets for avoiding bedtime? We may need a refresher course, but people half our size know those tenets well and use them effectively.

The following kid's guide to avoiding bedtime was compiled with the help of tired parents and young insomniacs. May it help to enlighten you as night approaches.

Afraid

This is the big "A." Parents sympathize with any kid who's afraid because they've been afraid before too. The bigger your eyes are when you come into their room, the bigger their compassion.

Bathroom

Always works. No parent likes the thought of a wet bed.

Can't Sleep

Not terribly effective. The usual response is to tell you to lie quietly with your eyes closed, or to approximate something that so closely resembles sleep there is no discernible difference.

Drink

The old standby. This works well, but usually only once per night (unless you've all eaten pizza).

Emergency

The word "emergency" works wonders. The problem arises in that what is an emergency to you differs greatly from what is an emergency to your parents. Some parents consider great bodily harm or life and death to be the only true emergencys, not social phone calls or botched hair styles.

Forgot

"I forgot . . ." can get you out of bed only if what you forgot is important to your parents. Brushing teeth or homework may get you a slight reprieve, but forget about the unfinished video game.

Gum (in Hair)

Gum in the hair will get you out of bed and keep you out for some time, especially if your parents can't find the scissors. Somehow, though, gum appears most frequently in your hair after 6 A.M.

Hungry

Some parents are very concerned that their kids not go to bed hungry. Your best chance to show how hungry you are is to ask for raw vegetables or cottage cheese— not ice cream. The shock itself may be enough to delay bedtime for half an hour.

Itch

Itches are a good summertime excuse, especially if you have mosquitos or poison ivy in the area. The time it takes to find an effective remedy in the medicine cabinet will be considerable.

"Just This Once"

A good phrase to remember in unusual circumstances. If a classic movie is on, a special friend is over, or a distant relative visits, see if you can stay up "just this once."

Kiss

What parent can resist the request for one more goodnight kiss?

Light (vs. Dark)

Bedtime can be drawn out or delayed indefinitely by a discussion of why your bedroom is either too dark or too light. The time spent increases exponentially depending on the number of siblings who share your room.

Monsters

Works well for smaller children (also see "A"). Parents will often look under your bed, in the closet or in any of the various places you suggest to reassure you. This can also be a lot of fun.

Nightmare

Guaranteed results (also see "A"). The only catch is that you must first go to sleep in order to have a nightmare.

Ouch

Often when you lie quietly for a while those places you bumped or scraped during the day may suddenly come to mind. Use them to greatest advantage.

Pray

If your parents forgot to pray with you this may bring them in your room, but it won't be much help in getting you out of bed again.

Sick

Be careful. Remember, sick people go to bed. Vague symptoms may keep you up for half an hour provided you have no fever.

Temperature

Any kid knows if you're too hot or too cold it is easily fixed by adding or removing blankets. But pretend you don't know this. Good for a short reprieve.

Undress

Very slowly. Parents don't like to see kids sleep in their clothes.

Video

Few parents let their kids stay up late just to finish watching a video. But since you may have more success staying up to watch educational videos like National Geographic, guard your viewing habits carefully.

Walking

Sleepwalking is better than an excuse to get out of bed. It is getting out of bed. The

Quick

If you have not yet gone to bed but are being summoned, look intently occupied by whatever you're doing, sit on the edge of your chair and say, "I'll be done really quick." Do not take your eyes off your project when you speak. It should gain you a few minutes.

Remember

What you remember is very important (also see "F").

It is best to remember something your parent must do: bake cookies for tomorrow's bake sale, call the principal or accompany your class to the zoo the next day. In the ensuing confusion, bedtime can be completely forgotten.

problem is, you can only really sleepwalk when you don't know you are sleep-walking. Be-cause you don't know you're doing it, it can't be much fun. And if you do know you're doing it, you're not really sleepwalking. Somehow parents always seem to know the difference.

X-Ray

(Also see "E"). This is the perfect emer-gency. Any accident requiring an x-ray, like falling from the top bunk, will postpone everyone's bedtime.

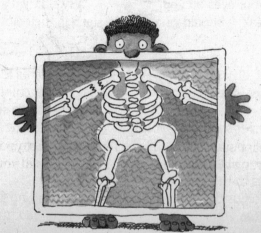

Yawn

Be careful. This is a sure sign that you are beginning to lose the battle.

ZZZZZZZZZ

Always remem-ber in the face of defeat, there'll be another bedtime to avoid tomorrow.

"Please stand by. You have temporarily lost your picture.
Broadcasting will resume when you have finished your homework."

"When you come to something sticky, don't charge me for it. It'll be my son."

To Yell the Truth

("Did I tell you about the time Daddy . . .")

Mom on the Loose

I was finding my involvement in a prison ministry program very rewarding, but my 4-year-old didn't always appreciate the time I spent away from him.

One afternoon I hurried through my grocery shopping with him so I could get to my volunteer commitment. The check-out line was long and the store crowded. It was at that moment that he complained loudly, "Mom, I don't want you to have to go back to jail today!"

ROSALIE TURNER, CLINTON, MISS.

Daddy Training

Kenny was struggling with potty-training and with each successful endeavor would get resounding applause from his father, mother or big brother. One day, while company was eating at their home, Kenny's father excused himself and went into the rest room. A moment later, Kenny threw open the bathroom door and yelled, "Clap for Daddy. He did it right!"

LAURIE DENSKI-SNYMAN

Future Shopper in Training

As a toddler, Troy was a challenge to take shopping. On one of my brave attempts, we ventured into Bartons, a children's clothing store. As I looked through clothing racks, Troy was busy himself. I found him walking toward me with his pants pulled down to his ankles. He shouted, "I goed potty, Mommy!" Being in the process of toilet training, he was quite proud of himself.

I quietly wondered and worried where he had accomplished this feat. Taking me by the hand, Troy led me to the shiny potty chairs on display. On our next visit to Bartons, we noticed the potty chairs were now kept on the highest shelves—beyond the reach of toddlers.

ELLEN SCHUKNECHT, BEND, ORE.

A Bit of the Bubbly

One morning I woke up with an upset stomach. By afternoon I had begun to feel better and started sipping on a cola. At about 5 P.M. the phone rang and my young son answered. It was a friend inquiring about a ride to our ladies' Bible study, which met that evening. My son promptly told her that Mommy was sick, but she'd had a few drinks and now was feeling better!

JANE REYNOLDS, CHARLTON, MASS.

The Best Policy

My 8-year-old daughter and I promised to each other that we would always say what we felt. This pact took an embarrassing turn one day when the pastor's wife asked if I had enjoyed her gift of pickled beets.

"They were wonderful," I said courteously.

With an astonished look on her innocent face, my daughter dutifully corrected me. "But Mom, you said they tasted like your old running shoes."

BONNIE J. LOVELAND, MEMPHIS, TENN.

Running on Empty

Six-year-old Molly came into the kitchen where her mother was fixing lunch.

"Mama, I have a stomach ache," she complained.

"That's because you haven't eaten yet," said Mom. "Your stomach is empty; you'd feel better if you had something in it."

That evening the minister stopped by for a visit and happened to mention that his head had been aching all day.

"That's because it's empty," Molly piped up. "You'd feel better if you had something in it."

SARA JO HANSEN, GRACE, IDAHO

125

"It took a while . . . but I finally got the kids to bed."

About the Authors

Joan Wester Anderson, who lives in Arlington Heights, Ill., raised five kids and lived to tell about it. Her last book, *Where Angels Walk: True Stories of Heavenly Visitors* (Barton & Brett), made the list of religious bestsellers.

Marti Attoun, mother of three, recently retired as feature writer and humor columnist for *The Joplin Globe*, Joplin, Mo., to make time for cooking and sock-sorting.

Dave Branon is a father and free-lance writer living in Grand Rapids, Mich. He's also a writer and editor for Radio Bible Class.

Darleen Hainline is a free-lance writer and home-school teacher living in Jonesburg, Mo. She and her husband have four children.

Karen Harter lives in Portland, Ore., with her husband and two children. She's a veteran of the real-estate business, but probably has more fun when she's writing.

Sharon Hinck, mother of four, somehow finds time to publish articles in *Baby Talk* and *Marriage Partnership* magazines, among others. She lives in Minneapolis, Minn.

Nancy Kennedy, a free-lance writer, finally celebrated the new decade by buying a fax machine. She lives in Inverness, Fla., with her husband and two children.

Mark Tabb is pastor of First Baptist Church in Springville, Calif. His wife and three daughters are willing participants in basketball games and outdoor expeditions.

Ron Wheeler publishes cartoon strips and tracts from his home in Kansas City, Mo. His strip, "One Bigg Happy Family," has been a part of *Christian Parenting Today* for the last three years.

Sally Wilkins lives on a farm in Amherst, N.H., with her husband. With five children under 10, she has plenty of writing inspiration.

Jeanne Zornes, a frequent contributor to *Christian Parenting Today*, is a mother of two and a free-lance writer living in Wenatchee, Wash. She has written for and edited books and magazines since 1970.

Christian Parenting Today is published bimonthly in Sisters, Ore., by Good Family Magazines, a division of David C. Cook Publishing. If you liked this book and want more laughs (and some real parenting advice), contact CPT subscriber services at P.O. Box 545, Mt. Morris, IL 61054, 800-238-2221.